ODES TO TOOLS

Dave Bonta

For the veined octopus (Amphioctopus marginatus)
and the biologists who documented its tool-using behavior

ISBN 978-0-9781749-9-6

Cover photo by Dave Bonta
Designed and published by Phoenicia Publishing, Montreal
www.phoeniciapublishing.com

First Edition printed in the United States
January 2009

PHOENICIA PUBLISHING
MONTREAL

Contents

ODE TO A SOCKET WRENCH

Better than all power tools
is the socket wrench:

its accommodating nature
its chrome-plated steel
its handling of torque.

It can make a complete revolution
from the smallest arc

& as if time could turn
in either direction
with the click of a lever

the past screwed down
the future loose

a spring-loaded finger
clicks against
the gearwheel's teeth.

ODE TO A CLAW HAMMER

Back when all angels were male,
the hammer was the first
perfect androgyne.

Mounted on a pegboard,
it still looks almost aerodynamic,
poor thing.

This is no claw, but a pair of legs
strong enough between them
to give birth to nails.

Or rails that forgot to run parallel,
converging on a vanishing point
that's much too close:

the train's stuck in station
& the hammer keeps trying to hop
on its one flat foot.

ODE TO A MUSICAL SAW

No longer walking
the straight & narrow,
no longer restricted to the harsh
amens of service,
now it's your turn to be held still

for the sawing of some
effete bow, generations removed
from any kinship with arrows.
But you're free!
And this song of yours

might otherwise
never have been heard.
You put your whole body
into it, still ascetic,
but now for the cause of art.

There's a sweet spot, the street
musicians say, & they find it
in you. Where the heart might be,
systole & diastole in perfect balance,
if you were more than cartilage.

The pure tone floats up
through two octaves of rejoicing
at your deliverance
from lumber.
Or is this grief?

ODE TO A HAND TRUCK

Eohippus of the truck family,
divergent offspring
of wheelbarrows,
what led the hand truck
to stand on its head
& press its nose to the ground?
What could it possibly
have learned from the worm
& the tons of dirt
that pass through
a worm's stomach?
How to let fall, perhaps,
boneless as hope.
How to take its time.
Stack truck,
sack truck,
bag barrow,
trolley,
it tips backward with alacrity,
trusting in vinyl grips
& ball bearings.
Its faith moves refrigerators.
Like a rowboat, it makes
its pilot also
face away from
the direction they're going:
blind faith must be shared
in order to work.
The job over,
I return the hand truck
to its spot under
the barn forebay,
between the Ford dump truck
& the old wheelbarrow,
no longer red, on which
so little
now depends.

ODE TO A SHOVEL

Digging with a shovel
always makes me hungry.
It's too much like a spoon, I suppose,
& the soil too close
to food here: heavy, brown,

& as full of foreign objects
as any stew. The shovel
is both tongue & tooth
on a white ash body
twice as big around as a broom.

I love groundbreaking,
holding the handle out like
a dance partner, momentarily solemn
until the first absurd little hop
onto the top lip of the blade

& the fast ride down, barring
a sudden & jarring contact
with rock or tree root.
I love cutting sod
& setting the shovel aside

to worry the dirt free from each clump.
I love giving the earth
a new — if temporary — mouth
& listening for the harsh syllables
of rock on steel.

I even like jollying the blade
around some impediment
that threatens to snap the handle,
feeling the thing budge & loosen
& at last let go,

& the shovel cradles
its unlikely prize,
sharp-edged & slick with charisma:
a tool nobody's invented
a use for yet.

ODE TO A HATCHET

This hatchet hasn't bitten
through a neck in twenty years.
When we raised poultry
it was in weekly use,
& also had regular dates
with the bench grinder:
a grating hiss, & a bright
new smile would open
in century-old rust.
The back of the head flares
into a hammer,
lending heft & balance
to this almost-cross
& making it easy to hang
from a pair of nails.
In a museum in Pittsburgh
I saw a hatchet
that was also a peace pipe
with a bowl opposite the blade
& the handle drilled out:
a two-faced tool for political campaigning.
Whether depriving one's opponents
of their fleshy skullcaps
or making the circuit
of a smoke-filled room,
its true role was to mime death,
to undergo burial,
should diplomacy demand it,
its windpipe stopped up with dirt
in a grave shallow enough to allow
quick disinterment.
A sacred thing, meant to circle
from role to role.
A hatchet can even carve
its own next body,
the model for which —
as Confucius once pointed out —
is always frighteningly close.

ODE TO SCISSORS

A pair of old jeans —
I amputate both legs
with a pair of scissors.

¤

I've cut myself on paper,
on grass blades,
even on certain sharp words,
but never with scissors.

¤

One on a shelf in the basement
beside the string,
another with the craft paper,
& a third nestled in the sewing cabinet
among spools of thread:
We are rich. We have three pairs of scissors.

¤

Every schoolkid grasps
the concept of a balance of powers
thanks to fist rock, palm paper,
& peace-sign scissors.

¤

Mothers worry about
leaving their children unattended
with a left-handed pair of scissors.

¤

The raccoon going through
the new trash on the riverbank
is delighted to find a shiny orphaned half
of a pair of scissors.

❑

When I come into school wearing glasses
for the first time,
the other kids show me what I look like
by peering through the handles of their scissors.

❑

I'm walking as quickly as I can,
stiff-legged,
mindful of the scissors.

ODE TO A BUCKET

As a bucket ages,
its galvanized surface
takes on the look
of new ice — that blue-
white jigsaw puzzle —
or a flock of cranes.
Something in its make-up
clearly rebels
against its type-casting
as a mere container
or temporary conveyance.
Even half-full,
for example, the handle
cuts into the hand.
People rarely think
to store a bucket
upside-down, so when
the bottom rusts through,
it can at last retire
& start life over:
a planter
for marigolds
on top of a stump
in a crew-cut lawn;
a transportable target
for rifle practice;
or hung on a nail
in the garden shed,
a home for wrens.
They line it
with grass & weeds
& perch burbling
on the rim,
bobbing up & down
on spring-loaded legs,
drawing from
an inexhaustible well.

ODE TO FORKS

Metal claws of the beast
we would much rather
be descended from —
no wimpy swinging in trees,
no equivocating opposable tine —

whether pitching hay or turning soil
their purpose is the same:
to bite what they cannot chew
& carry what they cannot keep.

There are forks also in roads,
in creeks & in tongues,
but for them
everything remains open.
How ironic then that the man-made fork
should epitomize inflexibility:
insurrectionary bedfellow of the torch,
stoker of digestive fires,
guard's goad in an underground
we hope never to descend into,
minimal lightning that we are,
tree gone wrong.

ODE TO A MAGNETIC SCREWDRIVER

If the part that screws
is the head — this X-
shaped tip — then
the other end must be
tail: the shaft rooted
in transparent sun-
colored plastic like
an insect in amber.
And considering how
the power drill
with screwdriver bit
has replaced it,
this might as well be
a relic from
the Mesozoic.
The tip attracts
anything steel, but
can only solve for x,
descending into
the head of the screw
like a spirit
into someone possessed,
spinning like a purpose-
driven whirlwind
in a desert of wood,
inclining ever so slightly
toward magnetic north.

ODE TO A PLUMB BOB

Brass doorknocker
for a house without a door

downward dog
always on point over the same
obvious quarry

flightless rocket
leaded with failure

pendulum made
to mark eternity
one still moment at a time.

ODE TO A HOUSE JACK

This time, there are no magic beans.
Every man-jack turns into
an acme-threaded beanstalk.

The hound under the porch
noses at the growing
hoard of sunlight

as the old house
climbs groaning
into the sky.

ODE TO A MEASURING TAPE

Tape that doesn't stick, reliable as the pronouncements of some close-lipped neighbor who never goes beyond the corner of the block. Tape that bends to follow the flank of a fish. Vacuuming dried begonia petals from a window ledge, I accidentally suck up a snail shell, one of three I'd had on display. It rattles briefly down the long hose & is gone. Shall I open the Shop-Vac's fat belly & dig for it in the slag heap of dust & dead beetles? No, I'll look for another. Snails in the woods are subject to continual Rapture — their empty shells are legion. Ditto for the ladybugs that litter every corner now that winter is past.

In an old house like this, nothing is square. The yellow blade of the contractor's measuring tape was out of its case more often than it was in, checking the height of the ceiling every few feet. *Either come in or stay outside,* our exasperated parents used to tell us. On rainy days we'd spiral from the basement to the attic, leaving half-finished sketches to go try on costumes from a huge carton of old clothes.

Tape that doesn't stick, like the tongue of snake. I had a friend in grade school who particularly enjoyed this game of dress-up. We'd switch between oversized suits & oversized gowns without a second thought. One time we even dressed as a newlywed couple & paraded downstairs to show my mom. I don't recall her sharing our enthusiasm. As far as I was concerned, it was adulthood we were parodying, not gender roles per se. We laughed to think what kind of fop such clothes would actually fit. But now I can't fit into my own jeans from five years ago, & as for my erstwhile friend, some neighbor said he came out of the closet as a homosexual & moved to Florida with his lover, not necessarily in that order. I know if I were gay, I'd leave this area and never look back.

Tape that doesn't stick. Yesterday morning I wrote 25 lines, dense with slant rhymes & alliteration, & in the evening I retracted them & left just two words on the page, a fragment of an ode:

Steel
snail.

ODE TO SCYTHES

The scythes are emissaries
from a country
that no longer exists.
They have only each other
to converse with now
that their translator
the whetstone went off
& joined the knives.
They huddle together
in corners, nested esses
long in the tooth
but still as fluid
as the staff of Moses
at the exact moment
it shifted into an asp.
Do you remember,
they murmur, how
the crowds
would lose their heads
& stand like soldiers,
stiff, when the wind
moved through?

ODE TO A PLANE

1.

The carpenter's plane glides
through a sky of wood,
no propeller but the knob,
no tail but the tote,
no landing gear but the mouth & the blade
& no chance of flying but the flat steel frog.

2.

The carpenter's plane touches down
& down. Chips curl in a wave
that never stops breaking.
No one ever really escapes;
all planes are bound to the planet.
The only route out leads farther in.

3.

When the carpenter's plane got to Japan
it began to work in reverse:
there's always more power in the homeward pull.
You go out hungry & come back
digesting fragments light as air,
dangerous with the scent of new surfaces.

ODE TO A SPIRIT LEVEL

Who would have thought that two vacant globes
preserved in alcohol

could so hold a construction
worker's attention,

a devotional gaze otherwise reserved
for gravity-defying breasts or buttocks

if not always the eyes that go with them,
that cool disregard

that elicits a squint & a whistle
at whatever fails to fall into line.

ODE TO A HOE

What begins with this
singular *L*?
New worms, certainly,
from the splitting
of their parent self.
Whole new cities
of aerobic bacteria.
Stones from rocks.
Sprouts of pigweed, lamb's-quarters,
purslane, dock: seeds
that had lain dormant for decades
until the hoe stirred them
into life.
This italic *L* spells
hills for yams,
channels for irrigation water,
a level bed for flowers.
Its thick tongue
uncovers an instant palate.
Luh, it says.
Luh luh luh luh.
The shocks travel
up the aching arms.

ODE TO TIN SNIPS

Scissors with an overbite,
blades like quotation marks
devouring the text —
some lost codex from
the Aluminum Age —
& leaving in its place
a jagged rent: massively
buck-toothed myself,
I know how elusive
a clean break can be.
Despite what orthodontists
would have us think,
a naturally straight bite
is a rare thing.
Most of us learn early
how to compensate,
squaring the circle,
holding our heads over
whatever plate, baring
our lips in the inevitable
tin grin.

ODE TO A CHALK LINE REEL

The day after Bo Diddley died, I watched a carpenter stretch a line the length of a board & give it a pluck: a diddley bow with no reso-nator, dry chalk instead of a bottleneck slider's glissando note. I'd been expecting blue, but this line was red. The saw followed shortly with its howling eraser.

I had an argument with the carpenter about new tools versus old. Why does something that works ever have to be replaced? Why red? Why plastic for the housing? Why the constant upgrading to new drills & saws? The carpenter showed me his hands: they were cruelly crippled. I can only use what fits my grip, he said.

That sudden, electric blue from my father's chalk line was one of my favorite things. Inside the chrome-plated reel I pictured a Galilee of chalk where the string went to renew its glowing shadow, like a blueprint line translated from the plane of the ideal: fuzzy, but straight as a fault.

ODE TO A CROWBAR

Comma, apostrophe, back-
slash, cursive flourish —
an all-purpose divider
that only accidentally resembles
a question mark in search
of its dot-like perch.
No self-respecting crow, beak
clever at leverage, ever
departed from
the declarative mode.
Male & female
hand & handle,
heavy as Wednesday.
What iron tree might ramify
if you insinuated yourself
into some sidewalk crack?
I know that curl
from watching seeds sprout:
cotyledon at the point
of pulling apart.

ODE TO A COPING SAW

Perhaps because it is flexible
& maneuverable

or because it has as many teeth
as a school of piranhas

or because it relies on a pull
rather than a push

or because it prefers circles
to straight lines

or because it excels
at impromptu reconstitution

or because it encompasses
so much empty space

somehow
it copes.

ODE TO A HIVE TOOL

You need a key for entering where there is no door.
You are much too full of your mammal self
to fit through the always-open entryway
& in any case would have no idea
how to execute a waggle dance,
which looks like sun-drugged madness to you,
looming over the brood box with your angry halo.

You need the hive tool — a burglar's jimmy —
to prize the honey-heavy frames
from the super, where they hang
for all the world like file folders,
an archive of everything that blooms.

You bring your smoker, of course,
stuffed with straw you pilfered
from some poor scarecrow.
With tear gas & face shield you come,
gloved & booted,
walking gingerly as a boy with his first erection,
praying for the insurgency to die down.

ODE TO A COMPASS

I can still recall
my first encounter
with a compass in
the second grade.
It was shiny & dangerous,
a headless ballerina
with one wooden leg.
How odd, I thought,
that we should entrust
the drawing of circles
to something so asymmetrical.
And what to do
about that pinhole
at the center of the paper?
It seemed flawed
& unnecessary, like a seed
for a stone. I wanted
a way to make
a circle from without,
like shaping a pot
on a wheel. I had seen
hawks spiral
around an updraft
with nothing more
than a slight adjustment
to the wingtips.
Shouldn't we
who are descended
from the trees
be able to free-hand
perfect circles,
simply by letting
the mind go blank
as a target?
The compass is a crutch.
Restore its missing leg
so it can return to
its first life as
a gnomon:
stationary,
circled by the sun.

ODE TO A SHOEHORN

A shoehorn's a sort of
spoon-shaped chute
for the foot,
not for the shoe.
Or at best, a social lubricant
between the two,
with or without
the Freudian interpretation.

Boots are for those
who toot their own horns,
sporting as we know
the handy bootstraps,
which give the so-called
self-made men
a better metaphor for rising
to their own occasion.

ODE TO A WIRE BRUSH

Never was walking
a greater penance
than for one without any feet
& legs more numerous
than the corrosive rain.
And the to-&-fro of it:
pacing is a refuge
when you can't stand still.
Do it long enough
& distraction turns into discipline,
the ground warms
& acquires the hard gleam
of an interrogator.
You confess, confess, confess.
Your tracks are covered
with a thin brown dust.

ABOUT THE AUTHOR

Dave Bonta is official poet-in-residence, personal chef and general dogsbody at the Plummer's Hollow Nature Reserve in Central Pennsylvania, though he is nowhere near as handy as these odes might suggest. In fact, he is a managing editor of the online literary journal *qarrtsiluni*, and his favorite tool is the computer mouse. Born in 1966, he is just three years older than the Internet. He began writing poetry at the age of seven, and has had poems published in such diverse places as *Art Times, Birdwatchers' Digest, Frogpond, Bamboo, Pivot, Studies in Contemporary Satire, The Sun, Poetry for the Masses,* and *Wind*. His photos have appeared in *Cha, Sawmill* and *Woodlot*, the New Hampshire Public Radio website, and the second edition of the college textbook *Insect Behavior*, among other places. The poems in this collection originally appeared as a series on his personal blog, *Via Negativa*, from April 4 to July 24, 2008.

www.ingramcontent.com/pod-product-compliance
Lightning Source LLC
Chambersburg PA
CBHW071807020426
42331CB00008B/2417